THE LONG AGO
AND ETERNAL
NOW

To Leonard Cohen

Bill Lewis

THE LONG AGO AND ETERNAL NOW

Poems

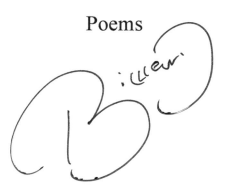

Greenheart Press

First published by Greenheart Press in 2017
Greenheart Press is an imprint of WOW Kent
magazine
wowkent.co.uk

Typesetting by A Stonesthrow Design
Produced by The Choir Press

A CIP record for this book
is available from the British Library

ISBN 978-0-9571829-2-9

Author's Acknowledgements

The following poems appeared in various journals and anthologies:

The Isle is Full of Noises was published in 'Judicious Heretics' (Wordsmithery, Medway).

The Blackbird is the Author of My Day was published in 'Outburst' Eire and 'International Times' (Stride Press).

Neither the Otter Nor the Song Thrush was published in 'International Times' (Stride Press).

Thanks

I would like to give a big thanks to those who have generously helped with the publication of this book, especially my dear friend, publisher and editor, Emma Dewhurst. Also, thanks to Edith Bugilimfura, Ann Welch, Michael O'Connor, Sarah Hehir, Nathalie Banaigs, Elaine Gilbert and Chris Clark for their friendship, donations and encouragement in various forms, and to Ann, who makes all things possible.

Contents

All images are by the author

Foreword

Bill Lewis is a founding member of the Medway Poets, a group of poets writing and performing in the 1970s at the heart of the Medway Scene. For me, a relative newcomer, this period was an interesting time in the cultural history of the towns but less vital than the music and art actually happening in the pubs, cafes and streets around us. So, when I met Bill Lewis – I'd read his poems and learned of his legend – I wasn't prepared for someone so vividly living in the present. He writes, paints and performs with ferocious energy. I thought I knew what to expect from a poetry reading and then out came Bill with his shaman's drum and the character and charisma of a genius.

The poems in this collection are joyous: whether they are exploring myth in a distant land or a special offer on Chatham High Street, they shine a light on our souls and examine human nature with a brave tenderness that is heart-breaking and beautiful. Bill's work is deeply influenced by magical realism and although often rooted in Kent and the Kentish countryside, there is an element that embraces the wider world and journeys beyond reality into other realms.

The rhythm of his language is captivating. His poems read like songs to a cast of curious characters and the lands they live in. But always, lurking amidst the lyrical beauty, there exists a precarious moment that trips you up and makes you take stock – of yourself, of life and of how best to live it.

Never relax. Never feel that you know what to expect. These poems are playful; they carry with them a weight of knowledge and experience but they carry it so lightly. They are intensely sensual without ever forgetting that we are human and all the more fascinating for our imperfections.

Relish the superior cunning and wisdom of the animals that inhabit Bill's mind. Lose yourself in the worlds without and within, both carnal and imagined. And more than anything, take pleasure in the richness of history, mythology and meaning that make this collection so stirring.

Bill Lewis, the man, is as effortlessly stylish as his poetry. He loves Christmas. He hates board games. His wife Ann is the person who defines his life (and she dreams of bears). Being Bill's friend is intellectually stimulating (it's almost impossible to keep up) and heart-warming: you'll not meet a more generous man. Ask about him in any pub and you'll find the people of Kent have a story to tell. He's a poet of astonishing talent who has gathered a following across the world and yet remains, always, the true Medway poet.

Sarah Hehir, November 2016

Horse Flag

The horse flag flutters above County Hall.

        In the farmland and villages beyond,
The chalk horse in its grass green heaven,
        canters beneath fields,
          that are silvered by a lack of rain,
  and stretch further
        than geography allows,
Where dead fathers work
        disguised as scarecrows,
Their frames stuck together
        by sweat and straw.

The disused Oast
       harbours in its rafters
  white feathered phantoms
        whose yellow saucer eyes
Hold the image of dead mice.

        From my window
     I spy with my little eye
A place domesdaybooked
     and bramblepatched beyond repair.

The chalk horse gallops in a sky of grass
  amongst the scatterings
      of daisy and buttercup stars,

A stolen Anglo-Saxon banner
    battle-tattered in the church of the mind.

I was a Ten Year Old Dalek Killer

We fought Daleks on the asphalt
Of the school playground.
We stormed their city every playtime
Between the climbing frame
And the library in late 1963
In those weeks immediately
Following the assassination of JFK.

We fought the evil space aliens almost
Every day, only ceasing the attack
When the teacher rang the bell to
Call us back to our sums.

The Beatles sang *Love Me Do.*
Emma Peel wore a leather cat suit.
The world was black and white
And would not be in colour until 1969.

Our teacher, who had a complete set
Of Narnia books in the cupboard next
To her desk, said we could draw
The monster we had watched
In last Saturday's episode of *Dr. Who.*

We all drew the same thing.
It looked like a giant Venus flytrap but
With tentacles and eyes on stalks.

She taped them to the wall at the
Back of the class and everyone said
Mine was the best, but I knew that,
As at the age of five I had already
Told everyone I would be an
Artist when I grew up.

40 years later I watched that episode
On VHS and was surprised to see that
The creature is never shown.
We had all made identical pictures of
Something none of us had seen.

I was a ten year old Dalek killer.
With a *Man from U.N.C.L.E* briefcase
Complete with code book.
I had many notches on my Lone Ranger
Cap gun and it never ran out of ammo.

Music, Movement and Mime

In conjunction with
             BBC Radio schools programming,
                 each year a new songbook came out,
Containing lyrics and music
                     (mostly of folksongs,
                 sometimes sea shanties),
    with woodblock illustrations
                     of whirling weather vanes;
        or swirling leaf storms;
                             or windmills;
                 or farmyards;
        or milkmaids;
            or apple-cheeked women singing:
                Dashing Away with the Smoothing Iron,
                that seemed often to mirror the village
                     outside the school window
(I wonder now how different
             it must have been for city kids).

 In the big hall between
             the two classrooms
                         we danced
shoeless in our vests and shorts
                 upon the brown linoleum floor
        with its strong smell of polish,
    pretending to be Trolls
                     as *The Hall of the Mountain King*
        boomed from the art deco radiogram
        and our teachers did their best
                 to pull out the imagination
        that they hoped was
                 somewhere lurking inside of us;

6

except in my case,
                    where they tried,
          unsuccessfully,
                    to stuff it back into my head

and replace it with Maths and English.

Neither the Otter nor The Song Thrush

Not the otter,
              at home in two elements
     of river bank or
          in its sleek wetness of a world,
                         swimming through
          a black silken tunnel of water
                    as if flying in the firmament.

Nor the song thrush in
     wordless faith in its feathered being.
          .

Not the magpies who chatter loudly
     to each other, about who knows what,
          as they peer into chimney pots
               in search of juicy blue black bugs,
     And now, as I write this, are terrorising that
          Terror of a ginger tomcat,
               because he, in deadly curiosity,
               has strayed too close
                    to their home in our hedge,
     Outflanking him in a pincer movement
          as he bats them with his paw,
               turning this way and that,
                    until receiving a final peck at his rear
                    and realises he has bitten off
                         more than he could chew
                         and more than he
                         can bite off.

Nor the field mouse
　　who fears not the reaper,
　　　　although the combine harvester
　　　　cuts a swathe through her
　　　　　　　　cornstalk cosmos,
　　　　　its flashing blades
　　　　　spinning swastika-like,
　　　　　　threatening to end
　　　　　　　　　her little life
　　　　　　in a split second of steel.

None of these folk of fur or feather
　　　　　　　　of stream, of air, forest and field
　　have any need of such a thing as
　　　　　　　　morality.

Only man needs this.
　　　for he alone is
　　　　　the most inventive and
　　　　　　　　ruthless of all
　　　　　Death's helpers.

I Borrow this Gentle Sweep of Falling Snow

I borrow this gentle sweep
                    of falling flakes,
The hypnotic hush,
                    as they settle silently,
At first like black feathers
                    when seen on high against
                                the milky sky
Then closer to Earth as they pale
                            into significance.

I have missed this wordless white silence.

                            From whom do
I borrow this gentle sweep
                    of falling snow?

From a far better poet
                    with a wintery name.

Listen to the blank page
                    as it fills with snowflakes,
Like a New England wood
                    on a December midnight,
Seemingly as weightless
                    as a heavy inflection when
        put, with some skill, into a light conversation.

I borrow this gentle sweep
                    of falling snowflakes
That seek out and are finally caught
                    in a woman's dark eyelashes.

Autodidactic Poem

Even though I would
Sometimes like it, I
Find praise hard to take;

As if I am not entitled to
It or that it may come
With some barbed caveat.

Erudite?
                    Ain't that some
Special kind of glue?

No, I am not a scholar.
If I were I'd swear in Latin
Instead of Anglo-Saxon.
And fart in Sanskrit.

The Long Ago and Eternal Now

for Sarah Hehir

As I finish my second cup of coffee
The right people fall in love at the
Wrong time and the wrong people
Fall in love at the right time.
Some are castrated,
                    some exiled to convents.
While I eat my roast beef sandwich,
                heavy on the horseradish,
A woman is turned into a swan
And another falls asleep for a
                        hundred years
After pricking her finger
                    on a spindle.
As I push a wire trolley around
                    the supermarket
A white stag with seven tines
Speaks to a saint in a human voice
And a boy plunges into the sea after
Flying too close to the sun.
I buy a carton of milk, three cans of
Economy baked beans and a
Copy of the *Radio Times,* and the
Rememberer of Animals draws an
Ochre bison, outlined with soot
Upon the wall by cavelight.
A man crosses a bridge of knives.
A lost fire opal ring is found in the
                    belly of a fish.

None of these events make it to the
                    Nine O'Clock News.
Perhaps because we humans are
Strung between our personal
                    pasts and futures
Imagining them to be the present;
Whereas these things are
Happening beneath the heartbeat
Of the long ago and eternal now.

I got one of the cans of beans free
Due to a special offer.

Crows are the Anarchist Flags of Nature

A cacophony of Corvids.
A magical Murder of them.

Less unkind than a raven,
As unelected as any owl:
Crows are the
Anarchist flags of nature.

So black they cannot find
Their own shadows;
Last in the line when the
Voices were handed out;
They caw from the highest
Perches, on TV aerials,
Chimney pots and thin,
            bending branches
That seem too slight for
Their obsidian presence.

They can recognise
Individual human faces,
Hold a grudge for five years,
        some say, even count:
Crows are the
Anarchist flags of nature.

I watch them as they walk
Across early morning lawns,
Moving like little men
In tailed tuxedo jackets,
Only the top hats missing
From their formal attire;

Or pulling worms from the
Wet earth as if they
                    were noodles;
Or gingerly pecking at
Road-kill on the highway
While trying not to become
Road-kill themselves.

One of them outside
Sessions House in Maidstone
Spots a *McDonald*'s bag
Under a bench,
Circles it until the
                    litterbug has gone,
Pulls it out and holding
Down with one claw,
Cocks his head
In an almost human gesture.
Peering in, seeing the
Red cardboard carton
That once held fries,
His memory says *food,*
Ripping it apart
Only to find it empty,
Losing interest immediately,
Hops, flaps, and is gone.

I watch them up high,
Bowing three times
As they call.
Are they praising the wind,
Or calling for an
Errant partner?
          (they mate for life).

Crows are the
Anarchist flags of nature,
Last in the line when
The voices were handed out;
But to this poet
Their caws and croaks
Sound as sweet as any robin.

I Think Therefore I Might Not Be

A temporal tsunami
        that flattens the harbours of our histories.
Other versions are reflected
               in the hall of mirrors.
Our arrogance is no shield
            against the many worlds
   of retelling and remembrance.
              I feel the vast space open
Behind me, like sensing the
        size of a room through closed eyes,
The cold wind on my shoulder
          an icy draft caused by the door of
Memory being left open,
      or perhaps by the shifting of stage scenery.
Behind us the past rewrites itself,
          becoming myth,
             becoming poetry.

I am the sum total of things
        that may never have happened.

Insomnia

Insomnia is the
Lines of poems
That are like
Little red
Cartoon devils
Who poke
You with their
Pitchforks, saying:
Get up, get up
You lazy bastard,
And write us down.
Insomnia is
Death saying*:*
I was just
Passing and
Thought I'd look
In on you, don't
Worry it's not
Quite time yet,
But I will be back;
By the way
That pain in your
Bowels is not going
To get any better.
Maybe you should
See the Doctor.
Insomnia is you
Saying in your
Mind all those clever
Things you should
Have said but
Decades too late.

Then just as
The sun clears the
Rim of the Earth
And the blackbird
Starts to sing,
You drift off into
A deep velvet sleep,
And the alarm clock
With malicious
Mechanical glee
Rings and rings
And rings and rings.

The Blackbird is the Author of My Day

The blackbird sings
                my day into existence
At one moment operatic,
                then comic, then conversational,
Sounds he may have overheard and
        recorded in the feathered scrapbook of
                his blue-black head,
Lilting, punctuated by trills and hymn-like
                        crystal sharp chords.
He is its author, director and
        conductor of the orchestra of dawn.

I don't write these poems;
                it is the rain that types at a
Hundred and twenty words a minute with
        furious fingers
                upon my bedroom window
        on sleepless nights.
                It is the brown heat of summer,
The black trees seen against a sky
                in the yellow apple-sweet morning,
The green wind that ripples the seas
                        of wheat and barley,
Vast cereal oceans that stretch
        all the way back to my childhood.
It is your perfect thighs that I can't
                gaze upon for fear of going blind;
It is the moon where the
        stolen voices of owls were hidden by
Some goddess in
                the Springtime of the world.

It is the wind chimes in the garden;
                    it is the secret names of cats;
               it is the boundless joy of dogs;
    It is the starving child;
       the blind woman and the poor
                and the voiceless that write
                    these bastard songs:
                         these orphan lyrics.

The blackbird sings my day into being.
A day so strange and full of
          love and sadness and
                    frustrated desires that worry the
          tender flesh beneath my clothes,
                    that dry like sweat on my body.

Because what does a blackbird know
                    of the terrible needs of man?

From the Yellow Notebook

1.
Poems grow on the lemon tree.
Damn it, I wanted fruit!

2.
Yesterday I heard a colour
That I had not heard before.

When I tried to write it down
I could not hear it anymore.

3.
The mountain passes
Judgement on the
Music of the sun
    (those kind of things
happened all the time
in ancient Greece).

4.
In a mirror
This poem may appear
Closer than it actually is.

5.
Between the entrance
And the exit
Did you not think to take
A good look around at
This interesting room?

6.
High up in the cedars
Ravens mimic chainsaws.

7.
In my house: a shooting star.
In my star: a shooting pain.

1976: I

My first thought was:
The food in heaven is atrocious.

My second thought was:
And for some reason they've
Given us blunt knives and forks.

My third thought was:
Oh, I am still alive
I couldn't even do that right.

Then I smashed a glass ashtray,
To unpick the stitches

In my wrist, sending fragments
Onto the dinner plates of the

Three other patients at the table,
Ruining their dinners and

Adding selfishness
To my long list of faults.

1976: II

I remember kneeling
In front of a nurse
(Her name was Gina
And she had tight
Blonde curls and a face
Borrowed from an
Italian painting),
A bandage on my wrist,
As I handed her several
Sheets of A4, on which
I had written (as if doing
Lines in school detention)
I failed I failed I failed
I failed I failed I failed
500 times in small
Shaky letters in blue biro.

Outside the window
It was October and it
Stayed that way for the
Next three months.

Two Poets

I remember those
Young man's poems.
Bright black beautiful
Bastard words
With no father
This side of hell,
Shaped like crows
That flapped from
The ink into the air,
Searching for a
Tetragrammaton
To unmake a universe.
I remember those
Young man's poems,
That were like
Slamming doors,
The whoosh of
Whiskey tossed into
An open fire.
They raged and burned
In my notebooks
Until the pages scorched;
Then were beaten out
On typewriters until the
Keys broke like teeth
In a street fight.
I remember those
Young man's poems,
They are buried now
Under the many
Snows of yesteryear.

With each thaw the
Minutiae of existence
Was revised and edited;
Streets rewritten
So I could never
Find them to walk
Down again.
Now I write an
Old man's poems.
Each word a tear
For the frozen dove
On the iron hard earth
As I search the
Thesaurus for synonyms
That speak only of
Kindness and celebration.

The Other I: Lost and Found in Translation

1.
Just before he touched her there he remembered that
In English *garden* is an anagram of *danger.*

2.
In English you only need to rearrange two letters
to turn *scared* into *sacred.*

3.
Sue's French boyfriend started his letter to her:
Expensive Susan.
Her father said: *he's no idea how right he is.*

4.
Despite the word having only four letters in its English
version she thought it might still be too large to fit into
her petite French frame.

5.

A beautiful Iranian woman left a comment under my Facebook profile picture: *you are very handsome.*

I replied: *it is an old photo and even when I looked like that women were not interested in me.*

She wrote back: *then they were flavourless.*

6.

Luisa put the money into the slot but no parking ticket came out. She hit the machine with the heel of her hand and a long line of Italian expletives fired from her Loren-like lips in blazing crimson letters. John knew then that he wanted her.

7.

Jennifer looked at the photo and said, *Oh dear, I didn't realise I was showing so much thigh.* The word *thigh* sounded good in her mouth. Her tongue like a lathe turning the leg of some exquisite piece of furniture made from some light blond wood. I waited for her to say it again. She did not.

8.

My Dad came back from Ginger Manser's office looking like the cat who had got the cream. He had caught Diane, Ginger's secretary, adjusting her stockings. *She's got legs that go all the way up to her neck*, he said. To the ten year old me this sounded anatomically incorrect and highly improbable.

9.

Spain: Conchita's diphthong is like a stud piercing her tongue.

10.

Our words write the shape of our mouths.

11.

Cuba: She rolled her R's as she walked. Her walk had an adorable accent.

12.

She said, *you forgot how to use your hands as well as your mouth when you talk.*

13.

A bit of the other: a mid 20th century working class British euphemism for sex. I embrace the other not only in others but also in myself.

14.

The only place you can kiss yourself in a mirror is on the lips.

15.

Is a smile a physical thing or is it part of the personality made flesh? A bit of the implicate world made explicate. A rainbow bridge between the inner and outer you.

16.

A smile is the only kind of rainbow you can see at midnight.

The Other II: Fluidity, Shadow and Reflection

1.

He was typing the fourteenth draft of a story when suddenly, without warning, one of his characters said: *do you believe in the physical reality of angels?* Where had this line come from? He had not intended to write any such thing. He began to read through all he had written that day to find clues. Looking for footprints in the already melting snow.

2.

When the angels are near The Throne they take on male features but when they are in the proximity of The Shekinah they are feminised.

3.

At the height of your ecstasy it felt as if wings of fire were being pulled from your shoulder blades.

4.

We are all a marriage of triangles that make a six pointed star.

5.

In the West we have kept our sexuality in the same box that we keep our shadow. This can cause considerable problems.

6.

She is one of the nine daughters of Memory. Sometimes she has a yoni but at other times a lingam. She is always different but always the same. She says: *there is no poetry only The Poem.* She cuts the great poem with golden scissors and with each snip the poet dies a little death. She is one of the nine daughters of Memory pretending to be one person or another. When you gaze upon her she looks at herself.

7.

Vietnam: Ngyun sings of a bridge made of the wings of swallows whose wing tips touch and lovers cross to meet. She sings of a world that existed before Agent Orange, forests defoliated by napalm. A world that will exist long after the helicopter gunships are consigned to history; existing beyond the chatter of the monkey mind and the journalist's sound bite.

8.

Thailand: A Buddhist monk told me: *many Thai friends visit England but they find it an unfriendly place populated by ghosts who spend most of their leisure hours shopping or talking to bits of plastic.*

9.

The belly dancer's movements were liquid engineering. A patchouli powdered moon beneath a cloud of watered silk, below its pale curve a wet star. *Taste my couscous,* she sings, *bury your tongue in my perfumed couscous.*

10.

A disquieting thought nags at him: *is an excessive love of otherness just a mirror image of prejudice? Surely,* he thinks, *desiring someone because you find them exotic due to race or colour is not that different from hating someone for the same reason.*

11.

The Orientalist painters of 19th century Europe objectified odalisques, trapping them in prisons of worship. They were slaves twice over, first to the potentates who bought them in the slave markets. Second to the obsessions of the artists and those who bought their work.

12.

Notice, she said, as we watched the Flamenco dancers, *how the passion is restrained. As they dance it feels as if they want to touch, either to make love or to hurt each other, perhaps both, and yet they don't. The music won't let them.*

13.

Brazil: she sings as she dances past: *I am the one with skin like café con leche / that pours into the blue china cup of your eye / and I cried, yes I cried / when my samba ended I cried / when my samba ended the love I pretended just died.*

The Other III: Crossing Borders

1.
Is this a friendly visit or are you invading me?

2.
She said: *I am a closed state where infidels may not enter. The way in is where most men do not think of looking. The door is through my mind. My imagination is the deepest, most sensitive erogenous zone on my map. From its portal all of my rural, suburban and urban areas can be accessed.*

3.
All roads lead to me, she said, *not to Rome.*
All roads, as the Gypsies know, are inside of us.

4.
Their love was not an exact translation but more of a reconstructed poem.

5.

In the dawn of the purple crested hummingbird he kisses the eye of her turbulence. Her tropical mouth is a rainforest.

6.

He follows her coastline until he finds an estuary. He loves the pale dunes of her beaches and the gentle hills of her highlands. He reaches the source of her sacred river.

7.

They circumnavigate each other's meridians and cross time zones and barrier reefs. They follow songlines and dragonpaths on their skin, the silkroads of their legs; the spice routes from east to west, stopping for a while at each fertile oasis. Such passionate cartography, such arduous and amorous journeys.

Holy Girl

Salome was a holy girl,
I liked her more than I liked John.

She danced through seven levels,
Until she had nothing on.

Her thighs they were of Canaan
Her belly was of Babylon,

Salome was a holy girl
But those scribes did her wrong.

They reduced her sacred dance
With a writer's careless ease

Until Inana's dark descending
Was nothing but striptease.

Our Pockets are Full of Silence and Stones

We become ghosts by increment,
Gradually moving from the centre
Until we reach the periphery,
        leaning against the wall at the
Edge of the party, almost part of the
Wallpaper; or maybe in the kitchen
Where the wine and beer is kept;
Or, if we are lucky, sitting on the
Stairs talking with the only other
Guest that no one wants to talk to
Until we become totally transparent.

We become ghosts by increment.
Our pockets are full of silence and
Stones, and the safe of our heart
        has been robbed of its music.

The Gender of Time is Black

The gender of time is black.
I am caught up in her dance.
She wears a necklace of clocks.
From a distance they look
                    like human skulls.

A man paints his feelings
But instead we see a cornfield,
Where crows are startled
By the yellow hue of a sudden
                    gunshot.

The epileptic sun has an
Iron spike driven into its head.

The colour of time is female.

The Hand of Miriam

The thumb:
She loves me.

The index finger:
She loves me a little.

The middle finger:
She loves me a lot.

Ring finger:
She loves me to
The point of madness.

Little finger:
She loves me not.

In the palm of Miriam's
Hand is an open eye.

You are Always Never on my Mind

I could say that the tune playing on
The radio in the small café where we
Used to meet made me think of you.

Or that the way the woman at the next
Table inclined her head was so much
Like you that it brought a lump to my
Throat and I found my eyes were moist.

I could say that I followed someone
With the same colour hair as you,
Thinking that it just might be you,

Wanting them to turn around and not
Wanting them to turn around because
I knew that it could not be you in
That city; at that time; in that country.

I could say all of these things but
None of them happened because
I never stop not thinking of you.
You are always never on my mind.

Chambers

The heart is not infinite
        but there is still room for you.

Sometimes it seems as if
        it is Bluebeard's castle

With locked rooms where
        old lovers are chained.

You don't need a key and
        if you want to you can

Look in any chamber because
        you were always free to come and go.

No need to break down
        a door or shatter a window,

Only when you leave will
        the structure get damaged.

Lyric

She was an only child
      with a sister.
He was a quartet of one.
He placed a green dove
In the hollow of her hand
While she spoke of the horses
    in the heart of the sun.

They slept every night
In the library where
   all the books are made of fire,
And gave their allegiance
     to a man without eyes
Who played on a seven stringed lyre.

She was thirteen kinds of beautiful.
He was fourteen kinds of dead.
She brought him slowly back
   to life across the feather bed.

But one part of him stayed missing,
Thought cast into the Nile,
They looked but never found it,
Perhaps eaten by a crocodile.

Two Norths

My orientation
           changes like
The phases
           of the moon,
Like the eyes
           of the cat
In that poem by Yeats.

Sometimes I love
    the deep
           velvet valleys
But others
           the hot stem
Where white
           salt roses bloom.

My compass has
           two norths

But both of them are true.

Rain Dictionary

The town had the same name as
                    this town,
The streets had the same names
                as the streets in
                        this town
                but it was not
                        this town
        and the people did not wear
                    such bright colours;
        also the place was smaller
            yet seemed bigger than
                        this town.
It rained and we got drenched.
            I had to carry you through the
            flooded subway.
The flares of my denim jeans
                took years to dry out.
You bought me a dictionary and
                    wrote in it:
            for Bill, the day it rained
            so you can finally learn
                how to spell.
When I open its pages they are
                Still, all these years later,
                    full of rain.

I don't know where you are today.
            I hardly ever think of you.
                The book fell apart and
            I still can't spell.

Unavoidable Collisions in Time

The slow trajectory of lovers

      as they fall towards each other:

Sub atomic probabilities

      becoming inevitabilities

Until they reach
      sufficient velocity,

Coalescing into erotic probabilities

Becoming points of solidity
      on a path of least resistance;

Decaying trails of
      heavy objects in motion

Falling slowly through the sweet

      sad syrup of time until they finally collide.

The Model

(for TingTing Sung)

her eternal gaze into the lens
not at us but at a photographer
who is no longer there just
like light from distant stars
reaching our retinas
long after they went super nova,
posed in her inner occult mirror
overexposed in darkrooms,
exposed in expositions,
catalogued, digitised into
millions of pretty pixels
solarised and Man Rayed,
uploaded, facebooked
and instagrammed;
a dweller in the sepia cities
of a silver nitrate world.

Walking Together When Apart

I sew my shadow to
The soles of your feet,
A trick I learned from
Peter Pan's ex-girlfriend.

Where you walk, I fall
Upon the pavement
And sunlit wall alike,
Sometimes long while
At others almost gone,
When the sun is at
Twelve o'clock high.

Strobed by fence posts,
Lamp posts, hedgerows
And stands of trees,
A red flicker out of
The corner of your eye.

You talk to my ghost
And I talk to yours.
We are often together,
Even though only one
Of us is actually here.

Portrait of the Poet as the Fisherman's Wife

In the ocean there is
A boat shaped wound

Where sailors in white
Dress uniforms drown.

In my house of paper
I stare too long at the

Japanese woodblock print
And an octopus emerges
From its surface and tears

Open the watered silk of
My ultramarine kimono,

Its tentacles pulling apart
My limbs as it proceeds
To eat my shaved sex

As if it were a salty
Slippery sliver of sushi.

Sleeping Together

Sleeping together.
Not a euphemism
For anything,

Actually sleeping.

Like a two piece
Jigsaw puzzle,

       Yinyanged
Beneath the duvet

Like a season
Waiting beneath a
Snow drift.

Sleeping together,
Each in our own
Dream world

Perhaps interacting
With simulacrums
Of each other.
You, flying in a
Wooden airplane,
The pilot a bear
Wearing a leather
Flying jacket
And goggles
      (how I envy
Your sweet dreams).
Me, discovering

Secret rooms
In our house
And trying not to
Eat spiders.

Sleeping together
As we have
For decades,
In hotels,
On airport floors,
In tropical climes
Where cockroaches
Skitter and
Parrots and monkeys
Call in rainforests;
Or in a motel
On the edge
Of Route 66
With the desert
Of the southwest
Stretching beyond,
Where
     coyotes call.

Where
     coyotes call

Where
     coyotes call.

Sleeping together
In France
     Italy
        Holland
            Spain

Denmark
The USA;
Through decades,
on islands
in forests,
on mountains,
At home
In our
Blue painted
House in the
county of the
White horse,
In these towns
Of ship builders
And flying boats;
Sleeping together
On frosty nights
When the
Curious moon
Peeps through our window,
Casting its silver gaze
Along the books
On our shelves,
Squinting to read
Their titles,
Then, before it wanes,
At the two
Grey-haired heads
On the pillows.
Sleeping together.

Thesaurus Rex

Rex!
Here boy.
Good dog.
Sit.
Read the
Book.
Read the
Book.
I said
Read the
Book!
Look,
I know
The Proust
Was a
Bit difficult
But this
Is only
    Treasure-bloody-*Island!*
A twelve
Year old
Kid could
Read that.
Rex,
Let go
Of the
Book!
Open your
Mouth!
Don't
Eat the
Book!

Cat Poem

Who me?
I didn't do it.
I was not
There.
Not guilty.
Prove it.
Got a description?
Pointy ears,
Yellow eyes,
Black fur.
Could have
Been a
Million others.
In this street
Alone there
Are several
Who match.
Fingerprints?
I wish your
CSI guys
Luck with that.
No fingers,
See?
I was minding
My own business
Just squeezing
Through some
Bars or walking
Along a wall
No wider than
A tight rope.

Jealous?
Admit it.
Hey want to see
My impression
Of a hungry
Human baby?
I'm a natural
Thespian.
Got the looks.
Who me?
You must have
Me mixed up
With two other cats.
Maybe the
Dog did it.

Cat Poem 2

Call me *Ishmael*
               if you like,
I don't mind.
           I've been called
Much worse.
         Lately I've been *Jasper*
 Alias *Eric*
          AKA *Caspar*,
Balthazar,
        and on occasions,
    even *Fluffy* and *Tiddles*.
If I were human
          I'd have a drawer full
Of fake passports,
         like a spy or a hit man.
Recently I've been
             Grimalkin
To that nice old lady
         on the edge of town,
And *Pyewackit*
To that elegant woman
          with green eyes
(greener than mine)
      who likes to
         draw chalk circles
On her floor at midnight
And croon,
    Pye, pye, pyewackit and sing
         strange songs to me.
But no one knows
       what I call myself.

Above my Pay Grade

Do you like this crown of thorns?
I won it playing dice. Of course

The Centurion got the coat.
Typical, officers have all the luck.

Not sure if I want to wear it though.
How much do you think I'd get
For it if I took to a pawn broker?

Oh, here we go again, I must go,
Another trainload of prisoners.

I have to escort them to the showers.
I have no idea what this is all about.

Above my pay grade, but as they
Say, *Ours is not to reason why.*
Anyway, surely those in
Command know what they are doing.

Sharkheart

Behold this man,
He looks in every
Outward aspect
A human being.
But should some
Surgeon seek to
Crack open the
Cavity where his
Heart should be,
Instead they'd see
A Great White Shark
Swimming in
Hungry circles.

Behold this man,
This multimillionaire
Who will say: *I speak
With the voice of
The common man.*
And those who are
Trained to think
Only in black and white
Will believe it true.

Behold this man
Who will rise
To the top of any
Organisation until
He becomes CEO
Of a Multinational
Corporation but
Will not rest there.

Soon his steely
Gaze will turn to
Politics and that
Inner shark will want
Launch codes
On the menu.

The Hour of the Torn Curtain

The black sun casts
                a white shadow
At point zero when
                the curtain is torn.
The Mother of Owls
                walks at noontide
In a blaze of bleached
                sand and gasoline,
Circling the perimeter of your
                Abracadabras.
She knows the name
        of the angel that dances
                on the bullet's tip.
And that other that is
                written on the scroll
    you carry in your mouth,
        like a pebble to
                ease your thirst.
The black sun casts
                a white shadow
In the offices of
                the lost hours,
    where silence falls like
                a fine dust, and in the
    occult weather stations
                all activities cease.

At the moment of the white scream
        in the field where
                steel bayonets grow
        like obscene flowers,

When creation mourns every
       bug squashed against the screen;
In the rooms behind
         clocks and mirrors, the
    ghosts of ghosts
           curate exhibitions
     of love and atrocity
        and feed strange fish,
   as everything waits
       for the second to split.

Poem for the Untold Millions

To all those who died in
        The War to End All Wars,
And the countless others
        who died in the wars that came after
        The War to End All Wars,
To the many who died in the undeclared wars
        before and after
        The War to End All Wars;
To the peasants and students who were
        disappeared
        in the *dirty wars* that came after
        The War to End All Wars;
To the writers who were
        censored by the red pencil
        of Death;
The scientists who
        never made discoveries
And also those who died indirectly
        because of wars;
And those who died and yet
        their bodies lived on;
And those who in peace time were wasted;
Those who sweep our streets, and stack the shelves
        and do those low paid
        unskilled jobs
But perhaps have potential for greatness;
And those who are deemed great
        (when perhaps they should be the ones
        that sweep our streets and stack the shelves):

I promise that I will never
    see an apple as *just* an apple,
        a tree as *just* a tree
            or a man or woman as
                just a human being.

Expletive

I am told
That the
Worst
Swear word
In English
Begins with
C and ends
With *T.*

Although
I don't
Like to
Use bad
Language in
My poems
I also
Believe in
Calling a
Capitalist
A capitalist.

A Short Walk in the Interior

1.

I follow my own tracks into the interior.

2.

The horizon retreats. The sky is as persistent as doubt.

3.

The Director said: *It is important to know where you place your horizon.*

4.

A character in a movie said: *I keep getting caught up in my own history.*

5.

I see mountains dreaming they are clouds. I see clouds dreaming they are rain. The sea is in love with sky and reacts to its many moods.

6.

The woman asked: *why am I beautiful?*
Because you are loved, I replied.
The woman asked: *why am I ugly?* .
    I answer: *Because you keep looking in the mirror.*

7.

Shapeshifters know that shape is a matter of perception
not fact.

8.

When asked, the coyote said nothing. Later he sent me
a postcard on which he wrote, *Maybe you should talk to
a fox.*

9.

The fox said, *You really must stop taking a machine
gun into your dreams.*

10.

In the Jardin du Luxembourg, my friend Lucile
Davingnon spread her tarot cards.
I did not recognise any of the suits in this pack. The
Major Arcana was even stranger. One picture card was
The Queen of Bicycles; another showed a cat playing a
lute, its title was: *The Knave of Christmas Trees*. I
picked one that was face down. Turning it over I saw it

was the *Ace of Umbrellas*. This told me nothing. Although later it rained.

11.

I sat in a park and waited for The Four Marx Brothers of The Apocalypse. They made me laugh and because of this for awhile I thought I was a Marxist.

12.

A book told me that if I met Buddha on the road I should kill him. I did this and worried that I might be a psychopath. A psychiatrist told me that if I was worried about it then I wasn't one. I thanked him and then killed him.

13.

They say Buddha's last words were: *Don't build any statues of me.* I guess he didn't say them loud enough.

14.

There is more than one path to enlightenment. Anyone who believes there is just one does not understand the truth of metaphor.

15.

My wife only calls me Bill when she is cross with me. I
rarely call her Ann.

I would love her even if her name was not Ann.

Meister Eckhart said: *Stop flapping your gums about
god.*

When you love someone you hardly ever call them by
their given name.

16.

A conversation at the Eselen Institute between a Nobel
Prize winning polymath and a physicist:

— So, you think everything is made of probabilities?

—Yes.

— So everything is a metaphor?

— If you put it like that then, I guess so.

— So what are they metaphors for?

They thought about this until one of them, I am not sure
which, said:

*—Everything is a metaphor for one great central
metaphor.*

They sat in silence thinking about this until a second
question emerged:

—But what is IT a metaphor for?

After awhile the answer came:

—It is a metaphor for itself.

17.

Once we realise that everything in life is metaphorical, we can slide between one set of metaphors and another. This avoids unproductive conflict.

18.

A wise man once told me: *It is better to be kind than to be right.*

19.

Sometimes I forget to be kind. Then I remember and it is like coming home after a long hard day.

20.

We confuse words like *serious* with *solemn*. We have forgotten the difference between *beautiful* and *pretty*, two words that exist at opposite ends of a vast spectrum of meaning. One is easy on the eye the other as terrible as an angel. We mix up Ego and Self at our own peril.

21.

Imprecise language frays the edges of ideas.

22.

Long ago in a galaxy far, far away, Luke Skywalker, a lion, a tin man and a scarecrow walked over the rainbow to Asgard (or so a small white dog told me). At least, I think that's what he said, as I speak Wolf better than I do Dog. It gets so crowded here sometimes and everyone wears more than one mask.

23.

The fox said: *one of the worst things that can happen to you is being stuck in an elevator with a saint.*

24.

Blasphemy cannot hurt a deity. It can only hurt the thin skins of those whose egos tell them they are the only ones with the right to interpret truths. Rabia (a female Muslim saint) is shown carrying a firebrand in one hand and a jug of water in the other. She said: *I have come to burn away the rewards of heaven and to douse the torments of hell.*

25.

Every country on Earth is the greatest country on Earth. We suffer from the colour blindness of the compass. Some stupid men told us where to find the east and the west and like fools we believed them.

26.

Crossing the desert I met a beautiful naked youth riding a white horse. In some versions I shoot the youth and take the horse. In other versions I shoot the horse and take the youth. I can't remember which actually happened but you can't remember every mundane detail in your life!

27.

The fox said, *I don't like the title of this piece of writing that you've put me in. Maybe you should call it something else. I hear eponymous is a very big name in literature.*

28.

I spent some time in a psychiatric ward as a patient. I also worked in a warehouse and was at Art College for one year. I met a lot of mad people... but then, that's warehouses and art schools for you.

29.

Extra! Extra! Read-all-about-it! Read-all-about-it! Blackbird discovers 13 ways of looking at a poet!

30.

He might have been a young Native American on a vision quest but actually he was a 33 year old Jewish mystic called Yeshua ben Miriam of the House of David. After fasting for four days his own shadow rose up and said, *You don't have to do this, just turn these stones into bread.* If you fast in the wilderness your shadow will say things like this. He told his shadow to get behind him. That's where a shadow *should* fall.

31.

I meet a green man carrying an axe in one hand and a holly bush in the other.
— *I'm lost,* he says, *I've been stuck here for dark ages.*
—*You're in the wrong poem, mate,* I say.
Then I give him directions to Camelot.

32.

Eventually I catch up with myself and find me still following my own tracks.
—*Is this some kind of circle?* I ask. The *me* that I have been following replies:
—*I think so.*
I need some distance from this indecisive person. I walk away.

33.

The further I walk away from me the more like myself I become.

The isle is full of noises

Prospero and Ariel welcome us
Above the portal to the BBC.

We Hyperboreans wear raincoats
All year round, just in case.

At 221b Baker Street a US tourist
Complains about the lack of fog
And the scarcity of Hansom cabs
In Twenty First Century London.

Down the rabbit hole and on the
Other side of the mirror the living
Chessmen make their moves guided
By Number Two and Number Six.

I use a blue balloon and pretend
I am a cloud to fool the bees.

Peter peers through Wendy's
Window and finds she has aged.

A plane returns from a 1000
Bomber raid over Germany.

In Technicolor and monochrome,
The pilot wonders if in the next
World he'll have wings or a prop,
Wings or a prop, wings or a prop...

The red bleeds back into the rose.
Be not afeard, the isle is full of noises.

Chinese New Year in Chatham

Today if the map said:
Here be dragons,
It would be true.
There are dragons
And lions dancing and

Between *HSBC*
    and *POUNDLAND,*
The nature of Monkey
Is irrepressible.

Between *BURGER KING*
    and *PRIMARK,*
The Tao that can
Be explained
Is not the true Tao.

Between *BURTONS*
    and *DEBENHAMS,*
The mandate of
Heaven is in place.

The procession
Ends at Military Road
Where the Mayor of
Medway makes a speech
In which he manages
To confuse China
        with Japan,
The polite Chinese
Pretend not to notice.

It's Chinese New Year,
Our February,
    and bitterly cold.
The dancers in
    pink satin shiver.

A woman standing
Behind me in
The crowd says,
I don't know why
They don't do it
When the weather
Is warmer.

La Chansonnière

She confesses to the mirror
And to the Nation.
Which is just another kind
Of reflecting surface.

She confesses things a
Devout Catholic does not
Even tell a priest; that
A good Communist
Would not tell a commissar:
Naked songs of raw love
Wrapped in a
Blue, white & red tricolour.

She confesses in
The language of Descartes
That is also
The language of Surrealism
That is also
The language of
       Abelard & Heloise.
Precise yet passionate.

She confesses everything
That happens between
       five and seven.
She confesses for the
Fallen sparrow and
The fallen angel.

She confesses for herself.
She confesses for all of us.

Marcel Proust on Facebook

Zut alors!
I just dipped

A Madeleine
In my tea.

The Many Deaths of a Surrealist

He was hit by
                    a stationary car
Doing speeds
                    in excess of zero.

Died in a train wreck
                    caused by an ant
Crossing the track.

Perished in a fire
                    caused by trying
To smoke a painting

That he had mistaken
                    for his pipe.

Savaged by an
                    Andalusian dog.

Mauled to death by a
                    blazing giraffe.

His distraught wife
                    in an interview, said:

You Abstract Expressionists
Don't know how easy you have it.

Klezmer Poem 2

Quit your
Kvetching
Already,
Said the
Violin to
To the
Clarinet.

Always
You make
With the
Oy oy oy.

But the
Clarinet
Just laughed.

Not an eye on a Metronome

Kiki of Montparnasse
                was not an
                        eye on a metronome.
Kiki of Montparnasse
                        was a cello.
Kiki of Montparnasse
                        was not from
                Montparnasse.
Kiki was born in
                        Châtillon-sur-Seine.
Kiki was not Kiki when she was born.
Kiki was Alice Prin.
The river Seine *was* **The river Seine**
                                when she was born.
During the war
                she worked in a munitions factory
Where they built dirigibles
                        and assembled

                        grenades.
After the war she
            # EXPLODED
BOOM!
                like one of those **grenades**
Onto the Paris Art scene.
She watched
        ## *Surrealist FIST FIGHTS*
She posed,
                painted
                        and danced like a flapper
                through the **mad years**

94

Through coffee fuelled discussions,

Affairs & manifestos of the **heart.**

Kiki of Montparnasse was
                Muse and Mus-
                        -ical instrument
In the mind of Man Ray.
Kiki of Montparnasse was a

naked cello.

Kiki of Montparnasse
                was not an eye on a metronome:
That was someone else that
                        Man Ray loved.

Mars

A smoke-like dust devil in the
                    Amazonis Planitia.
        Shrinking mesas
                    in the south residual cap.
Frosty dunes in autumn.
        Dark sand atop periodic bedrock ridges in
                    Schiaparelli Crater.
Irregular shaped impact crater,
            with ejecta thickened by
                    sublimated ice.
Dust fans emerging from
                    cracks in the seasonal freeze.
A twenty mile carbon dioxide
                    frost avalanche
    in a scarp on the edge
            of the north polar layered deposits.
Seasonal changes reveal
                    details in the gully alcoves of
            a crater in the northern plains;
                    wind blown sand ridges
        above old channels carved by
                    water or maybe lava.

The stars above do not twinkle.
                    It is a world without birdsong.
There are no
            dark they were and golden-eyed.
No one for a
            Martian to send a postcard home to.
Nor is there a perfect copy of
        Green Town, Illinois in some long ago October.

Broken Journey

With this ticket you can break your journey,
Says the ticket collector to the woman
Seated opposite me.
I want to tell her that I
                once broke my journey
And it hurt;
Not as much as when I broke my ribs
When I fell in Chatham High Street,
Not as much as when a man broke my nose
By headbutting me in the face
                in a bar in Maidstone in 1975;
However the broken journey did hurt
And it left a scar half a decade wide
That never completely healed
That I have learned to live with.

Managua Notebook (1989) I

The East German alarm clock,
Bought in Bluefields,
That treats the actual time
As if it were a state secret.
The crunch of cockroaches
Beneath our feet on those
Nocturnal trips to the toilet.
The oscillating desk fan that
Sounds, through our light
Sleep like cars passing on
A rainy British street.
The Iguana that lives in the
Space between the warped
Wooden ceiling tiles and
The corrugated zinc roof,
Emerging each morning like
A dinosaur from a cave and
Scattering the roosting birds,
And sometimes clashes with
Some other creature that lives
In a corner of that same space,
Showering our bed with
Falling dust and insects.
Our landlady Doña Gladys
With her blue black hair
And oriental eyes, that might
Be from indigenous Indian
Blood although she swears it
Is from a Chinese ancestor;
Her body big and magnificent
As she moves like a cloud in her
White night dress, through the

Rooms of the house, where
Marianella, the 15 year old girl
Sweeps and cleans,
Wearing her sandals with the
Bright coloured plastic letters
Across the toes that spell
I Love Miami: a place as far away
From here as OZ is from Kansas.
She asks us what snow is like
And thinks we are kidding
When we say it is like the
Inside of Doña Gladys's fridge
When it needs defrosting.

Managua Notebook (1989) II

In the gleaming white
Air-conditioned pyramid of
The Intercontinental Hotel
A private party is in progress.
Dance music spills out into
A night sticky as quince jam.
Just up the road there is
A Sandinista army base
Where two sentries (man and a
Woman) guard the gate.
They tap their feet to the
Music, then one of them
Puts down her Kalashnikov
Leaving the box, motioning
To the other to join her in the
Centre of the street. He does so
And they begin to dance
Under the tropical moon;
An Hispanic Fred and Ginger
In olive green fatigues.

Managua Notebook (1989) III

Two off duty soldiers, a married couple,
Holding hands in the Plaza de España.
They are in uniform; olive green with
Red and black bandanas. They join us
In the queue at the stall selling *rojita,*
A soft drink that tastes like fizzy
Cough mixture. The female soldier
Notices the slogan on Ann's T-shirt.
It is a Chilean design from the days of
Popular Unity that says in Spanish:
Democracy in the Home
                    as well as in The State.
She smiles and digs her partner in the ribs
He looks at the slogan over the rim of his
Sunglasses, nodding in an *OK I get it* way.

Places

There is a grape
       on a vine, somewhere
             in the south of my thoughts,
That has my name
          written beneath its skin.

There is a café
          in a square, in a walled town
     at the foot of the Alps,
          that has an unwritten poem
     scrawled upon a tablecloth.

There is a glass of cognac
          on a table of a
Cross Channel ferry, my
          DNA kissing its rim,
That I left un-drunk,
          but may retrieve
       the next time I visit the 1980's.

There is a fishing port
          whose name in Spanish
         means *hope*
     that you won't find on any
          nautical chart,
Where racing cars drown
     and dead lovers are found
         in fishermen's nets;
Where every hour glass
        has a storm inside it.
I once stood there
        at night

Gazing out at the
                wine dark cliché of a sea,
      imagining sailors
               turned to swine by
          arcane women,
             and rumours circulating
     for dark ages
         until blind poets
            swept them up like potsherds
       and glued them into a story.

Visit That City

Visit that city.
Sit in its squares,
Sit in its cafes and bars,
Hear the bells of its
Churches and Cathedral.
Watch the painted
Wooden figures
Parade from its
Clock tower,
Marking the hours:
Bishop, Knight
Death and the Maiden.

Soak up the atmosphere,
Drink blonde beer
From a frosted glass,
Sip *café con leche,*
Or a chilled
Sauvignon blanc,
In the afternoon under
A sky of holy blue
When the sandstone
Walls shine with
Butter-yellow light
Dappled with
Blue-green shadows.

Visit that city.
View the paintings
In its museums and
Marvel at the worlds
Of dust that float in
The sunbeams that
Stream through the
Windows of its
Antique buildings.
In the heat of the
Afternoon, lie with
Exotic women,
The sun through
The venetian blinds
Tiger-striping skin,
As you caress their
Naked arms until
They shiver with
          languorous,
Indolent pleasure.
Or if you prefer,
With pretty boys
With smooth bodies;
I assure you they
Will react to
Your touch in
Much the same way.

Visit that city
And all the cities,
All the towns
And villages of
This interesting planet,
Because I don't
Have time enough
Left to see them.
There are so many
More places
Than I have years.
Read the books
That I can't,
Especially those
Not yet written,
Because there are
Even more books
Than there are cities.

Mare Nostrum I: Blue

I think I was looking for something just now
But I seem to have forgotten what it was.

Can you tell me, Angel?

Under which rock will I find
                    the sandals with wings?
Or the shield that
                reflects like a mirror?
Angel?
            Oh great, now you stop talking to me?!

Blue.   Bluer.   Bluest.

A continent of water.
                    An encircled sea.

Somewhere imbedded deep in this thing we call
'western art' is a woman standing by a window
looking out at a

Blue.   Bluer.   Bluest.
                    Deep blue sea.

Looking out ... or is she perhaps looking in?

Mare Nostrum II: Fever

The boy, born two months premature in 1953,
Attacked by the many fevers of youth.
A sickly child
               (when he was ten his mother said
In his earshot: *Is it worth teaching him anything*
Because he's probably going to die before he
                           gets much older).

The boy tosses and turns in the bed, the book
Having slipped from his hands
               (a copy of Charles Kingsley's
    The Heroes,
       2/- from a jumble sale at the
                    Sea Scouts Hut)
Beads of sweat on his forehead as he sails
Between islands inhabited by
               Ray Harryhausen
                    stop-motion monsters.
Armed skeletons sword fight with Jason.
A giant bronze man threatens to wreck the ship.
The giant Roc from the
               Seventh Voyage of Sinbad.
One phrase repeats in the child's head,
   the pleasant vale of Hellas,
          the pleasant vale of Hellas,
               the pleasant vale of Hellas.
He does not dream of growing up to be a poet,
Instead he is a Captain sailing in search
               of something,
     some undefined treasure.

Mare Nostrum III: Mission Impossible

Athena
          sends Perseus on a mission,
     a hit man with a contract
          to take out an earlier version of
                    herself.
Like an actress
          who has
                    gone legit
               and wants to destroy those
Porn flicks
               she made to pay the rent.
     Now she is
                    strictly classical:
     No room for that
                    Pre-Hellenic snake handling
                         primitive person
          from bronze ages ago.
                         A case of
Mythic disassociation
                    just as the Hebrews
          split
                    their god's psyche
          into snake and
                    Yahweh.

Mare Nostrum IV: Theseus

Theseus
        failed hero

But never the less:
        a hero,
Having killed the
        creature,

Did no one think to tell him
That if you kill your Shadow
        you become it?

Now filled with
        bullheaded pride
Casts aside
        his female side:
Ariadne
  with her
      spiderclever,
        spiderstrong,
          spidersilk
  thread,
    that led
        him out of
the mindlabyrinthdark.

Theseus
           failed hero
so preoccupied
           he forgets which
sail to hoist
        causing his father's
          suicide.

Failure and success are two
    sides of the same gold coin

    and in bright sunlight
The hero-shadow has horns.

Mare Nostrum V: Menton

Sometime in that long night journey
As we slept in our couchettes
That felt like
        luggage racks
                for people,
Another passenger got on,
A woman who ate
                a raw onion, bread and cheese
And drank from a
                bottle of *Stella Artois*,
    the sound and smell
                penetrating our half sleep.
She had gone by the time we were
Woken by officials
                (yet again) wanting to
Check our tickets and passports.
                Then more uneasy sleep as our
        carriage rattled over bridges and
Through tunnels and farmland
                        and villages and
        towns and towns and towns and towns and
                cities.

Until then the nearest thing I'd had
                to a holiday was a day out
        by the seaside at Folkestone.
                Now here I was
                standing with this amazing woman,
                confetti in her hair,
        rice and shoes in my pockets,

Looking at lemon trees.
    Lemon trees!
      in the town square,
Having been on a train all night
    and breakfasted in the carriage
On wedding cake and
    a bar of fruit & nut chocolate
 as the sun rose over Menton.

Mare Nostrum VI: Nice 1981

While we waited for the
              Chagall museum to open
We watched the floor show.
Across the street under
              the shade of a lime tree,
Some rich brat had locked
          himself, on purpose, inside
Maman and *Papa's*
      chocolate brown Rolls Royce.
His grey uniformed nanny
Hammered on the car window
With her fists as he sat
          arms folded, poking out
His tongue in defiance.
Then he began to lean on the
          horn as she yelled, red faced,
Things that I am sure were not in my
          French/English phrasebook.
She's no Gallic Mary Poppins.

Then the doors opened and we
              enter a realm of
Crimson angels,
              Fish with pendulums,
Skies full of
              ticking clocks.
Yellow horses
              dine on violins,
 The bride and groom fly
              out of the window while
          drunken Russian soldiers

116

With their heads on upside down
    dance to the music of the fiddler
            perched up high on the
Rooftops of Vitebsk.

After an hour we re-emerged
Into the leaf dappled sunlight.
The Roller is gone and we both
        wondered what compromise
    was reached?
                what wall breached?

That's life: drama, comedy
And Art in the space of an hour.

Mare Nostrum VII: Talking of Homer

By that sea I sat down with the old poet.
He looked familiar but his dying had changed him.
We shared some olives, goats cheese, broke bread
And drank some golden Retsina that we had kept cool
Hanging by a piece of string in the icy spring that
meandered down from the hillside
Until we felt we had a pine forest
growing in our mouths.
He fished in his pocket then asked,
I don't suppose you have a couple of coins on you?
I just want two. I think I may need them soon.
Then he told me how he had
Once met the great Homer, *Blind he was by then, but*
Able to recite his verse. I remember him sitting in an
Old armchair that he made look like a throne by his
Being there, his hands resting on the top of his cane.
He had the memory of a Funes, as he recited, to my
Surprise, not in Demotic Greek but in Spanish
With an Argentine accent. I didn't like his politics
but he was no doubt a great writer and the fact is
I owed him much.
I told him I had also seen that recitation on BBC TV,
A grainy black and white memory out of place here
By this shining interior sea,
still brilliant in the setting sun
As in the distance the
Ferry drew closer across the water.
I gave him two one Euro coins.
He looked at them in his palm for a moment.
Maybe it wasn't Homer, he said,
I don't always remember things correctly these days.

Mare Nostrum VIII: Perhaps a hundred years from now

You will have to find a village somewhere in the south of the world where they speak a language that's closer to Latin than German, and where there is a terraced hillside with olive groves, and further up on that hillside amongst the rocks, wild thyme and sage give of their sweet aromatic scents. It's quite a climb, I warn you.

Almost, but not quite, at the top of the hill, there is a house with a walled garden; its walls are yellow ochre but look pink at certain times of the day and hold the heat of the late afternoon as if they were hands of clay. This house has blue wooden shutters that keep the heat out in the summer and in during the winter, and are a joy to fling open in spring time, at dawn.

Before you see the house you may hear the barking of a dog. His name is Paris and he's a black Labrador as mischievous as the night is long. Don't worry about him, he won't harm you because he will recognise you easier than I; though be warned he can give a fearsome lick.

You don't have to knock at the door, just come around the back and I'll be waiting in the garden. I'll probably say something like: *you took your time.* Or I might just stand there and stare. After all, you will have a different face, and for that matter, so will I; but we will both know, won't we, that we are the people written about in this strange little story a long time ago by a poet long since dead.

We will have a lot of catching up to do, talking over all those old times that never happened; of people we never knew; wondering why he wrote this and brought us together; wondering if I resemble him in some way. Did he have a beard like mine? Did he, like me, drink red wine and read genre novels? Perhaps you resemble a woman that he knew, or maybe it was the other way around and *I* was the woman and he was you. Then I may start to laugh and you will ask me why, and I will reply:

He didn't give us any names. That bloody stupid writer. He even gave the dog a name, but not us.

Knowing you as I do, you will probably say:

It doesn't matter. As he is long since dead it might be that we are free to live our own lives in this beautiful house somewhere in the south of the world where they speak a language that's closer to Latin than German.

Mare Nostrum IX: Marseilles

She looks
           as French as
                         Nefertiti.
Her nose stud
                  is the morning star,
her nose a scimitar.

      She leans against the bar,
Feeding centimes to
                  the hungry jukebox,
 North African *Rai*
         then Serge Gainsbourg's
                  Reggae version of
 La Marseillaise
         now stripped of blood and
   guillotines by its Afro-Caribbean beat.

She looks
        as French as
                  Juliette Greco,
A hand of Fatima
        (or is it a hand of Miriam?)
                       around her neck.
  her mouth a *Ras el hanout* kiss.
The White Nile
        runs through her centre.

Outside the bar the mistral
                  blows south;
Silvery leaves
           rustle on the olive trees;
The wind speaks Occitan.

She could be the lady
            of whom the troubadours sang
    if not for the *Gitanes*
            that hangs from her bottom lip.

            West across the Levant
The *Khamsin,*
                    Scorpion wind,
            blows west,
    whipping up dust-devils like
                            Djinn
            released from the bottles where
Sulyman The Wise imprisoned them.

    Pernod.   *Suze* .
            Kir Royale.

    Signs that say you are still
                                in France.
    You need convincing in the
                harissa-red heat of summer.

She looks
            as French as
                        Nefertiti.
The African plate
            slides beneath her Aegean.
And in the
            The Calypso Deep,
                        Ionian profundity
    of her damson lidded
                        almond eyed gaze
You feel the tides of fado,
                        flamenco,

122

Sephardic romances
                and Sufi poems,
  And the intermittent
            signal of *Radio Tarifa.*

The Albanian merchant
            greets every Greek
                   or Turk
Or Italian or
    Spanish customer with:
              One race, one face.

The woman at the bar is
        as French as
              Nefertiti
With her blue-black hood of hair,
           a Cleopatra bob.

          And everyone here
   is as Greek as every Italian,
        as Arab as every Jew,
  as Moroccan as
          every Frenchman,
    Carried by the same currents
That drove Ulysses through the
          12 houses of the
   Zodiac
     (losing ships
        and men at every sign)
   While Penelope unpicked her
         Luna tapestry;
    Carried by the same currents
  as Marius in his sea-fever
       from a fictional version
  of this very port,

Where once a year the
           Gypsies carry the statue of
Kali Maria,
         Black Maria of the Languedoc
(of whom, some say
        is the daughter of
              Miriam of Magdala).

     And everyone here
Is as Greek as
        every Italian,
            as Arab as
                every Jew,
      as Moroccan as
          every Spaniard.

The Albanian merchant greets all with:
              One race, one face,
     one race, one face,
          one race, one face.

Mare Nostrum.   *Nuestra Mar.*

   Our sea.

Shaman Seeks Apprentice. Some Travelling.

for Elsie Hehir

A bear that is not a bear
Stepped out of the snowstorm
And into the village.

What do you want, Grandfather?
Ask the people there,
Because this is the way
To address a bear, especially
A bear that is not a bear.

I have come to take a boy
Who can not only read tracks
    In the snow but hear them.

There is no one like that here.

I have come to take a boy
Who will be the wife to a spirit.

There is no one like that here.

I have come for one who is
Not as graceful *as* a deer
              but *is* a deer.

There is no one like that here.

I have come for one who can
Speak caribou and
          understand caribou.

To translate for me when I
talk with the Animal Masters.

There is no one like that here.

I have come to take away one
Whom the spiders tell
        their silky secrets to.

There is no one like that here.

I have come for one who can
Unpick each octave
        of a wolf howl,
 And bend the
        wind and the star.

There is no one like that here.

Then with a knowing smile
The bear that is not a bear says,

Then I will stay here
        until one arrives.

There is a pause.

The village elders are in
Some consternation.

After some discussion
A boy is shoved with haste
From the door of his home.

Take him, grandfather
                    and go away.
Take him, grandfather
                    and go away.

He grabs the boy's hand
In his large clawed glove
And drags him off
                    into the whiteout.

I knew you were here,
It was in my dreaming, said
The bear that is not a bear.
You will not see this place
Again for many years.
When you return, you too will be
A bear that is not a bear.

I, Orpheus, being of sound mind, bequeath you...

I wanted to give you poetry
You only wanted rock and roll.
I would have given both to you
But no one would buy my soul.

I leave you with these things
I keep inside this box of bone
Some I have shared with others
But most are for you alone.

This is the buried acrobat,
This is the gentleness of knives,
This is the cast iron star
    I tossed into the sea,
This the torrential rain,
Her concubines and wives.

These were her Chinese blue
Erotic electric shadows
This is the coffee scented rose,
These are the stars
    like silver minnows,
These were the emperor's
    brand new clothes.
This is the sky-deep ocean.
This is the daughter of the
    bearded dream.
This is the mine shaft of midnight
Where we excavate the
    elusive seam.

This is the crooked sixpence;
Remember when
                    I walked that mile?
This is the poem that I never wrote.
This is my often unused smile.
Thank you for the gold watch
And the party that you threw.
Sorry I could not make it.
I came down with poet's flu.
Neither love nor sex can save you
When She sits upon your bed.
Her beauty takes your breath away
            and keeps you with her dead.
This is my last will and testament.
This is my stained and worn out suit.
This is the cup I have searched for,
The sweat, the salt, the open fruit.

Lightning Source UK Ltd.
Milton Keynes UK
UKHW012039020719
345426UK00001B/75/P